S
P
A
M
~
k
u

SPAM-ku

Tranquil Reflections on Luncheon Loaf

JOHN NAGAMICHI CHO

HarperPerennial

A Division of HarperCollins*Publishers*

HarperCollins books may be purchased for educa-
tional, business, or sales promotional use. For infor-
mation please write: Special Markets Department,
HarperCollins Publishers, Inc., 10 East 53rd Street,
New York, NY 10022.

FIRST EDITION

Designed by Nancy Singer Olaguera

Library of Congress Cataloging-in-Publication Data
SPAM-ku : tranquil reflections on luncheon loaf /
[compiled by] John Cho. — 1st ed.
        p.   cm.
    ISBN 0-06-095278-4 (alk. paper)
    1. Spam (trademark)—Poetry. 2. American poetry—
20th century. 3. Canned meat—Poetry. 4. Haiku,
American. 5. Senryu, American.
PS595.S767S63   1998
811' .54080355—dc21   98-29749

98 99 00 01 02 ❖/RRD 10 9 8 7 6 5 4 3 2

• CONTENTS

• ACKNOWLEDGMENTS

I would like to thank Alec Proudfoot for suggesting that I start a Web archive for these oddities of human/porcine expression. Little did we know how popular it would become (over 10,000 entries and counting)! Cgi programming by Screamin' Phil Erickson (and his crypto-wise-ass missives) have made my task as archivist much less painful. Thanks also to my editor, Jeremie Ruby-Strauss, for believing in the commercial potential of such absurdities, and to Ellen Rooney for the sublime illustrations. Finally, a big kiss for Colleen Kirby, vegetarian, for her love and understanding.

• DISCLAIMER

Many of the 5–7–5 poems in this collection are senryu rather than haiku. However, since "ku" means "verse" in Japanese, the term "SPAM-ku" is not a misnomer.

AMERICANA

1.
Perfection uncanned
Like a beautiful redhead
Fresh from her trailer.

2.
Ate three cans of SPAM,
But there's still room for Jell-O.
I *love* this country.

SPAM-ku • 2

3.
Mother's rough finger
Stirs water into the Tang
And glazes the SPAM.

4.
Easily yielding
To cowboy teeth. Soft and pink
As prairie oysters.

5.
June Cleaver, flummoxed,
Burns the SPAM roast. Wally says,
"Leave it to Beaver."

6.
Tropical SPAM night.
Suckling loaf roasting on spit,
Fake palm trees askew.

SILENCE OF THE PIGS

S
P
A
M
-
k
u
·
4

7.
In mud you frolicked
Till they cut, cleaned, and canned you.
How now, thou ground sow?

8.
Cold steel in a pig.
Clean up the blood, cook the flesh:
A pig in cold steel.

9.
Attach electrodes
To the SPAM, jolt it, shock it—
Still it will not oink.

10.
Someone please tell me
Do they have to starve the pigs
When making SPAM Lite?

11.
Practice SPAM voodoo.
Insert pins into pink block.
Somewhere, a pig screams.

ANTICIPATION AND DESIRE

12.
Sensing his need grow,
she knelt obediently
   and opened the SPAM.

13.
"Slow down," she whispered,
now guiding my trembling hands.
   "Turn the key slowly."

14.
I possess the key
To your tin chastity belt.
Open, breathe, glisten.

15.
It clings to the can
As I struggle to shuck it.
A porky oyster.

16.
The light in your eyes
When you hear the "beep-beep-beep"
    Of the microwave.

17.
    Succulent naiad,
I envy the warming oil
    In which you now bathe!

18.
Her bath is my broth.
The painted pork prostitute
Makes the water blush!

19.
In the Arab souk
skewers of SPAM entice girls
with silk-covered mouths.

20.
How my hands tremble
Applying a light coat of
    SPAM-colored lipstick.

21.
A bulge in my jeans.
"Is that SPAM in your pocket?"
    I blush and say "Yes."

22.
Leaning to kiss her,
Smelling her breath, I thought of
Love and luncheon loaf.

23.
My pieces are carved
From SPAM. Yours are of SPAM Lite.
Delicious checkmate.

EPIPHANY AND PORTENT

24.
    Moments of pleasure:
The small noise when the seal breaks
    When opening SPAM.

25.
    I felt a small thrill
When I nicked my ring finger
    On the can's sharp edge.

26.
Like a new piglet
Slick with slime, SPAM emerges
Making sucking sounds.

27.
Roseate pork slab,
How you quiver on my spork!
Radiant light, gelled.

28.
On my brown lunch bag,
A spreading translucent spot—
SPAM again today.

29.
Chew, puff, chew, puff, chew.
The cigarette gives SPAM a
Pleasant smoky taste.

30.
Flossing before bed,
I unearthed a speck of pink—
Hint of last night's SPAM.

31.
Whose powerful hand
Changed this empty can to a
Blue accordion?

32.
Kitchen windowsill.
Lit by passing headlights, SPAM
Casts a long shadow.

33.
You cut your finger
Slicing a loaf. Blood blossomed
On the snow-white board.

34.
The ceiling fan turns.
The loaf sweats ominously.
Time is running out.

35.
If a SPAM is burned,
Even bawds of euphony
Would cry out sharply.

36.
   Once, a fear pierced him,
In that he mistook his wife
   For a loaf of SPAM.

37.
   The storm clouds rolled in;
The winds roared around my house.
   I smiled. I had SPAM.

S
P
A
M
~
k
u
•
19

DREAMS AND NIGHTMARES

38.
In the cabinet,
It lurks, unseen, forgotten . . .
Then you move the soup.

39.
Gregor SPAMSA woke.
In horror he sees that he's
Now a pink pork cube.

40.
Fifty blocks of SPAM—
A giant PEZ dispenser
Crowned with a pig's head

41.
I once planted SPAM.
It reached long for the blue sky.
Victory Garden.

42.
Grizzled old tom naps
in the sun—*flick, flick,* his tail.
He must dream of SPAM.

43.
She dressed a pink cube
To look like me, and ate it.
Now my shoulder hurts.

44.
A billion SPAM loaves
Raining down from the heavens.
A pink dénouement.

OBSESSION AND ADDICTION

45.
Bought big block of SPAM,
Carved for days until I had
A small block of SPAM.

46.
A bulimic binge:
Bread, cheese, spam, chips, Spam,
SPAM, SPAM—
Gravity's rainbow.

47.
What a mockery—
Lettuce and fruits surround SPAM.
Why gild the lily?

48.
Oh when will SPAM cans
Display our lovely haiku
Printed on the back?

49.
Ruby rectangle
In a coruscating gel.
Jewel on my plate.

50.
My shoes have SPAM soles.
I wear SPAM jeans, shirts, and ties.
But my socks are wool.

51.
My friend is kosher;
She doesn't understand my
Passionate love, tears.

52.
Eyelids hang heavy
As father drones on and on
About its great taste.

53.
A madman, obsessed
by SPAM, screams, "Stop me before
I haiku again."

54.
They break down the door
As he opens the SPAM can.
The rabbi exposed!

55.
Bite once: it's just lunch.
Bite twice: it starts to entice.
Bite thrice: paradise.

56.
Through the wall I hear
My neighbor say, "What good SPAM!"
I burn with envy.

57.
Seven cans of SPAM
Stuffed inside my evening bag.
Now I feel secure.

58.
New brand: Chia SPAM.
Meat and greens in every bite.
Hormel, we'd buy it!

59.
Five, seven, and five
Are not enough to capture
The essence of SPAM.

60.
New group to combat
substance abuse: "MASH"—Mothers
Against SPAM Haiku.

IN ALL TONGUES

61.
Kuufuku desu,
SUPAMU o taberu.
Atogusare.

62.
Ist es nur das Fleisch,
oder wahrlich der Heiland?
Was ist diesen "SPAM"?

63.
O SPAMI vitae
Gloria in excelsis.
Volup labere.

64.
AMSPay aikuhay
Ogicallay Anguagelay:
Igpay Atinlay.

65.
"SPAM" in French is "SPAMME."
Like *SPAMME frites* and *SPAMME l'orange*.
The French are so cool.

66.
Vienna sausage
Was a product of the times—
SPAM de siècle.

TRAGEDY AND DESPAIR

67.
A man sits depressed.
A lone tear rolls down his face.
The key has broken.

68.
They have no more SPAM.
My hands tremble with anger.
Cleanup on Aisle 5.

69.
Romantic deceit—
She said she loved me, but left
　Once the SPAM was gone.

70.
I put my shoes on
But remembered far too late
　My secret SPAM stash.

71.
Made a SPAM puppet
To entertain my doggie.
Need a new hand now.

72.
Locked in room with SPAM.
Try to pick lock with can's key.
It snaps, I am doomed.

73.
Wore my SPAM boxers.
Struck down by a speeding bus.
Paramedics laughed.

74.
Memories of days
Waiting in employment lines—
Long days without SPAM.

75.
 Next-door barbecue.
Smell of T-bones waft over.
    Eat SPAM with closed eyes.

76.
 A half-eaten slice.
Ants swarm the cold, greasy plate.
    A suicide note.

SEX AND ROMANCE

77.
SPAM and PAM in pan:
"Meat" frying in "cooking oil."
Metaphor for sex.

78.
He proved his manhood
To the lunchroom girl with SPAM,
Swallowing it whole.

79.
SPAM smells so sexy.
A little behind the ears,
And I can date cops.

80.
I sent her eighty
SPAM haiku to show my love.
She sent me a shrink.

81.

At my confession:
"I love SPAM." "What, carnally?"
Hadn't thought of that.

82.

Autoerotic!
Open can, insert member:
Wham, bam, thank you, SPAM!

83.

> The man is ashamed
> To tell the prostitute what
>   To do with the SPAM.

84.

> Soft, pink, fleshy SPAM
> Goes from yonic to phallic,
>   Hardening with heat.

85.

These SPAM sex acts: Could
They be described as merely
    A poke in a pig?

86.

Alone, I stroke SPAM
And remember how you felt,
    You slimy bastard.

87.

Ma paled when I said,
"Pa gets into S & M!"
    I only meant S(PA)M.

NATURE

88.
    I hear the SPAM ball
It bounces—*porqua, porqua.*
    A haiku of spring.

89.
    A little sparrow
Beneath a picnic table
    Pecking pork pebbles.

90.
    Climbing an elm tree,
I found some SPAM on a branch.
    Serendipity!

91.
    Cooked over mesquite,
SPAM enrobes the desert moon
    In a fragrant stole.

92.
Savory pink block,
Like a deer at a salt lick,
 I give you my tongue.

93.
Sunset placid pond
Where campers often linger—
 Rusted can of SPAM.

94.
Rectangular plot
Of dirt among the grass blades
Where the can once was.

95.
SPAM autumnal hue
Deepens with the rising heat.
I hear leaves crackling.

96.
In the thawing snow,
The can's blue corner peeps out
   Like spring's first crocus.

97.
   Behind the aged cheese,
I find grapes growing wrinkled
   And SPAM with a beard.

98.
Hold tight, street person!
Wise-ass crow on the Dumpster
is eyeing your SPAM.

99.
SPAM needs no chewing.
It slides like fish down the throat
Of a cormorant.

100.
Black cat drags about
his pink, purloined bite of SPAM
like an extra tongue.

101.
Shooting star of SPAM,
Tail like a greasy white plume,
Gastronomical.

102.
SPAM volcano blows.
Stratosphere laden with pork.
Gorgeous pink sunsets.

ANTHROPOMORPHISM

103.
She sits on the shelf,
Cold, coy, pork product temptress.
"Sodium," she coos.

104.
Tap, tap, goes the spoon
On the metal can. Inside,
Is the SPAM dancing?

105.
I stare, it stares back.
I long to know its feelings.
It demurs. Lunch, then.

106.
Silken pig tofu,
The color of spanked buttocks
Blushing at my knife.

107.

I sing little songs
To help the SPAM stay cheerful
Until I fry it.

108.

Weep not, little SPAM,
Most humble of processed foods.
You have fed armies!

109.

My SPAM is in heat
Yowling like an alley cat
    Wanting a good fork.

110.

SPAM, too, needs a wife.
What consort for my Pork Prince?
    Ah! The Velveeta!

111.

Patio slime trails
Are not from snails but anxious
SPAM seeking escape.

112.

Bright lights and cruel cops
grill the suspect pork product.
It doesn't confess.

113.
Does SPAM contain tongues?
When you eat it, does it taste
    you as you taste it?

114.
The beach picnic ends.
The sand blows, the naked SPAM
    Puts on a tweed coat.

115.
Take a SPAM for walks.
It will gambol at your feet.
Salty-sweet plaything!

116.
Awoke to find I'd
Grown a SPAM upon my head.
It wants its own hat!

117.
Can of SPAM looks up,
Contemplates an airliner.
   Thinks, "It's just like me."

118.
Dangerous Dan SPAM,
Steel outside but soft within,
   Seeks saucy side dish.

PHILOSOPHY AND DEEP THOUGHT

119.
Descartes on pig parts
Says: "I'm pink, therefore I'm SPAM."
Deep philosophy.

120.
Translated Descartes
Into English, reversed; it's
"SPAM emoS," I think.

121.

"What meaning has life?"
The SPAM rests, mute in the chair,
Ignoring my angst.

122.

SPAM is pork shoulders:
Where is the rest of the pig?
Like one hand clapping.

123.
Bishop Berkeley says:
Even when we don't taste SPAM,
    God is tasting it.

124.
Bit into a chunk.
A continent somewhere sunk.
    All is connected.

S
P
A
M
~
k
u
•
67

125.

Veggie Hormel snack:
Spiced wheat germ, compressed in
blocks —
But who will buy SPERM?

126.

SPAM: it's a short word.
Takes a moment to say the
Monosyllable.

127.

Ingredients: pork
with ham, salt, water, sugar,
sodium nitrite.

THE ARTS

128.
Salvador Dali
Paints soft, drooping cans of pork:
   "Persistence of SPAM."

129.
   Cheeks pink as primrose,
SPAM-sculpted. Sweetly dimpling,
   Pigmalion smiles.

130.
"Form follows can," said
Walter Gropius during
lunch at the Bauhaus.

131.
Brasiliana.
Amorphously glistening.
The sound of SPAM Getz.

132.
Blanche to Stan: "I have
Always depended upon
The SPAM of strangers."

133.
Man wearing white shirt
Drops meat, causing greasy stain;
Cries, "Out, out, SPAM dot!"

134.

SPAMLET: Danish ham.
Lite version: HORMEL Gibson.
Cooked up by Bacon?

135.

What once contained SPAM
Now rusts in tall roadside weed—
Kerouac long gone.

136.

Clever Daedalus
Makes wings of SPAM and feathers.
At last, pigs can fly!

PHYSICS AND MATHEMATICS

137.
Split the SPAM atom.
Enormous pink mushroom cloud.
World covered in pork.

138.
You can never know
What it's like 'til you taste it.
It's Schrödinger's SPAM.

139.
    SPAM symmetry group:
Top bottom, left right, up down—
    Iso-tasty moves.

140.
    A SPAM slice frying
In the southern hemisphere
    Turns counterclockwise.

141.

How many degrees
Can one tilt an ungreased pan
Before a loaf slips?

142.

Mathematicians can't
square the circle. However,
Hormel can cube pigs.

VERSATILITY

143.
Waxed my car with SPAM.
The finish gleams, water beads,
   Hungry dogs chase it.

144.
I balanced the cans,
Then struck a pose upon them.
   The crowd was impressed.

145.
This bow tie of SPAM
Matches my pink cummerbund.
    What, is it too loud?

146.
    An empty SPAM can.
My boy makes a sea-blue boat.
    Its hold smells of pork.

147.
    Skeet shooting with SPAM.
A little more costly, but
    Look at that pink spray!

148.

SPAM slice in toaster.
Switch on, tie down ejector.
Pink, smoky blow torch.

149.

Childhood classroom game:
Poke straw through loaf, aim,
and blow.
Pork missiles scream by.

150.

I have some SPAM wine,
A nineteen-ninety vintage.
It's still quite lumpy.

151.
I fill my hourglass
With SPAM. The seconds go by:
    Splat. Splat. Splat. Splat. Splat.

152.
    Armageddon come,
I shall build my shelter from
    a million blue cans.

A LOVE EPIC

153.
Supermarket aisle.
We reached for the same SPAM can.
We exchanged numbers.

154.
You carved my figure
From the block of SPAM. Love or
Infatuation?

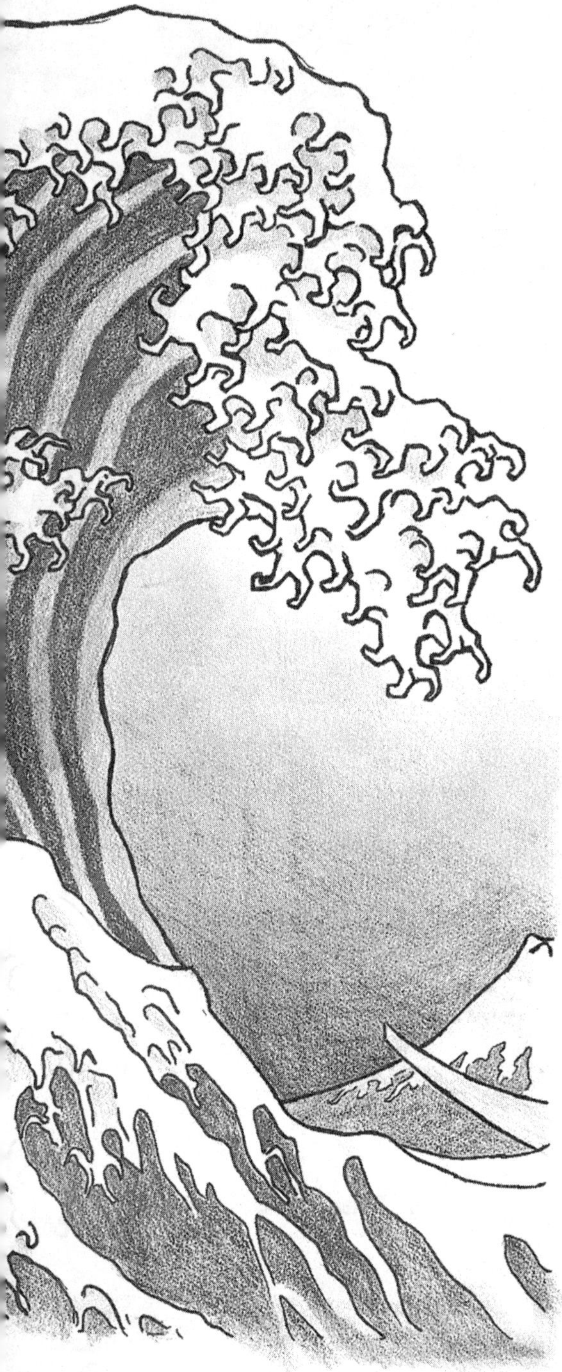

155.
The first time we kissed:
Your cheeks flushed a deep
    SPAM pink,
    Your lips soft, hungry.

156.
I buried the ring
Inside a loaf. You took a
    Bite, spat, then said, "Yes!"

157.

Honeymoon in France.
Finally got to try the
SPAMME frites, SPAMME l'orange.

158.

Four children later
We run out of things to say.
"Price of SPAM is up."

159.

"Breakfast in bed, love."
"What is it, dear?" "Refried SPAM."
You filed for divorce.

160.
The first nights were bad.
Woke up from a SPAM nightmare—
But you were not there.

161.
I live alone now.
I keep a cat for comfort.
She does not eat SPAM.

162.
Supermarket aisle.
I saw her reach for a SPAM.
I turned, walked away.

AUTHOR LIST

Brian Beakley: 120, 123
Deborah Benarosh: 19
Dave Bieri: 62
Martin Booda: 64, 132
John Nagamichi Cho: 2, 5, 6, 32, 33, 34, 35, 36,
    39, 44, 46, 65, 66, 75, 76, 77, 80, 102, 134,
    140, 141, 148, 149, 153, 154, 155, 156, 157, 158,
    159, 160, 161, 162
Tom Elliott: 10, 11, 21, 24, 37, 45, 48, 50, 70, 71,
    72, 73, 121, 126, 137, 144, 150
Phil Erickson: 131
Chris Fishel: 53, 55, 113, 119, 128, 142
Peter Fotopoulos: 101
Liam Friedland: 82 (coauthor)
Steve Garrigues: 74, 93
Michael Geraty: 109
Cissy Hartley: 68
Francis Heaney: 9, 16, 25, 28, 30, 31, 38, 52, 56,
    59, 81, 83, 87, 90, 94, 96, 104, 107, 125, 133,
    138, 151
Geoff Holme: 85
Mary Holt: 15, 86, 143
Tom Howard: 61
Jon Howell: 82 (coauthor)
Rex Jones: 22
Paula S. Jordan: 129
Michael Kalantarian: 13
Ben Kovitz: 14, 63
Dave Krider: 41